COMPARING DIRECTIONS

UP AND DOWN

by Tessa Kenan

TABLE OF CONTENTS

tadpole
books

UP AND DOWN

She is up.

He is down.

She climbs up.

We sit down.

yo-yo

The yo-yo is up.

The yo-yo is down.

He bounces up.

He bounces down.

She is up.

She is down.

He is up.

He is down.

Who is up?

Who is down?

WORDS TO KNOW

bounces

climbs

down

sit

up

yo-yo

INDEX